A Troop of

Chimpanzees

Heinemann Library
Chicago, Illinois

Richard and Louise Spilsbury

© 2003 Reed Educational & Professional Publishing
Published by Heinemann Library,
a division of Reed Elsevier, Inc.,
Chicago, Illinois

Customer Service 888-454-2279

Visit our website at www.heinemannlibrary.com

Designed by Ron Kamen and Celia Floyd
Originated by Dot Gradations Ltd
Printed in Hong Kong, China by Wing King Tong

07 06 05 04 03
10 9 8 7 6 5 4 3 2 1

Library of Congress Cataloging-in-Publication Data
Spilsbury, Louise.
A troop of chimpanzees/ Louise and Richard Splisbury.
    p. cm. -- (Animal groups)
Summary: Describes the physical characteristics, life cycle, habitat, and individual and group behavior of the chimpanzee.
  ISBN 1-4034-0746-0 (HC),   1-4034-3288-0 (PB)
  1. Chimpanzees--Juvenile literature. [1. Chimpanzees.] I.Title   II. Series

  QL737.P96 S645 2003
  599.885--dc21
                                    2002004038

Acknowledgments
The author and publishers are grateful to the following for permission to reproduce copyright material:
p. 4 Ann and Steve Toon/NHPA; p. 5 Peter Davey/FLPA; pp. 7, 26 Steve Bloom; pp. 8, 23 Kennan Ward/Corbis; pp. 9, 15, 16 Martin Harvey/NHPA; p. 10 (top) Wendy Dennis/FLPA; p. 10 (bottom) Nick Gordon/Oxford Scientific Films; p. 11 Steve Robinson/NHPA; p. 12 Konrad Wothe/Oxford Scientific Films; pp. 13, 25 Craig Stanford/Oxford Scientific Films; p. 14 Christope Ratier/NHPA; pp. 17, 18 Bruce Coleman Collection; p. 19 Andy Rouse/NHPA; pp. 20, 22 Gallo Images/Corbis; p. 21 (top) Adrian Warren/Ardea; p. 21 (bottom) Nigel J Dennis/NHPA; p. 24 Michael Leach/NHPA; p. 27 J. and A. Scott/NHPA; p. 28 Mike Birkhead/Oxford Scientific Films.

Cover photograph of a group of chimpanzees reproduced with permission of Steve Bloom.

The publishers would like to thank Claire Robinson for her assistance in the preparation of this book.

Every effort has been made to contact copyright holders of any material reproduced in this book. Any omissions will be rectified in subsequent printings if notice is given to the publisher.

Some words are shown in bold, **like this.** You can find out what they mean by looking in the glossary.

Contents

What Are Chimpanzees?

Chimpanzees, or chimps, are remarkable apes that live in Central and West Africa. An ape is a **mammal** closely related to humans and to monkeys. Chimps, gorillas, orangutans, and gibbons are all **species** of ape. Apes have no tail and their arms are longer than their legs. They are very intelligent.

Chimps have long hands and fingers, short legs, and are covered in black hair. Their faces have large **jaws** and ears. Their eyes face forward. Male chimps are slightly larger than females and have sharper, longer teeth. Most young chimps are born with a white patch of hair near their bottom. Their skin is lighter in color than adults' but it turns darker as they get older.

An adult chimp weighs about 88 pounds (40 kilograms). It is about 47 inches (120 centimeters) tall.

4

A Close Relative

Chimpanzees have a close relative, called the bonobo, that lives in West Africa. Although they look very similar, bonobos and chimps are different species. Bonobos are thinner with longer arms and legs. They have flatter faces, reddish lips, and longer hair.

What is a troop?

Every chimp is an individual. It looks and behaves a little different from other chimps. Most chimps spend some time alone doing things for themselves, such as finding food. However, chimps are also **social** animals. They spend most of their time doing things with other chimps in a group. A group of chimps is called a troop.

Apes' hands and faces are shaped like human hands and faces. Chimps and other apes can also walk on two legs.

5

What Is a Chimp Troop Like?

A troop of chimpanzees contains adults and young males and females. Different troops contain different numbers of chimps. Some groups are as small as 15 chimps, while others are as large as 120. Most troops have about 40 members. Most of the time, the chimps in a troop all get along with each other.

The members of a chimp troop are hardly ever all in the same place at the same time. They are usually scattered around in smaller groups or alone. If they meet up with other chimps from the same troop, they might form a larger group and look for food together. Or they may simply greet each other and walk on by. Chimps in one troop normally keep away from the members of other troops, with whom they often would fight.

Males and females

Adult female chimps stay close to their own babies and young chimps. Sometimes they also help to look after the young of other females. Females protect the young and help them find food until they are about eight years old. By then, the young chimps have learned to take care of themselves.

Adult male chimps spend a lot of their time alone or in groups of all male chimps. They do not help care for any young chimps in the troop. Males stay near the females only when it is time to **mate.**

This mother chimpanzee is taking care of young chimps in her troop.

Who is who in a troop of chimps?

In most groups of animals, including humans, there are leaders and followers. Leaders tell or show followers what to do and how to do it.

In a troop of chimps, there is one leader. The leader is always an adult male. He is called the **dominant** male. The reason he is dominant is that he has fought with other males in the troop and won all the fights. The leader can boss around all the other chimps in his troop. Even so, he helps them find food and always takes the lead in fights against other troops. Females in the troop prefer to **mate** with the dominant male.

There is a clear **pecking order** in a troop of chimps. Any adult male is dominant over any female. Older females are generally dominant over younger females. Young chimps are the least important.

In any troop of chimps, some are more important than others.

Showing respect

Chimps all look slightly different, so they can easily recognize other troop members. The way each chimp acts toward others changes based on how important the chimp is within the troop. These differences can be hard to spot. It may be as simple as a less important chimp lowering its head or looking down as it passes a leader. These are signs of respect. They tell the leader that the less important chimp knows who is boss.

Grooming

Chimps help keep each other's hair clean by using their fingers and teeth to pick out dead skin and **insects**. This is known as **grooming**. Mother chimps groom their babies. Most chimps only groom other chimps that are more important than them. So, young chimps groom adults and females groom males.

One way to tell which chimps are dominant is by watching them groom each other.

Where Do Chimps Live?

Chimpanzees are found only in certain parts of Africa, near the **equator.** They live in and around trees in the **rain forest** and **savanna.** In the rain forests, it is hot, and it rains almost every day. Many trees grow there and most are very tall. A savanna is a type of **habitat** where trees grow by themselves or in small patches of woodland, surrounded by large areas of grass. The weather is usually warm and dry, but sometimes there are short, heavy downpours of rain.

Animals that live in these habitats have special **adaptations** for living there. Chimps can see, hear, and smell very well, which helps them find food and avoid **predators.** Chimps have thick hair that keeps them warm at night and in wet weather. It also protects their skin from thorns and from the strong rays of the hot sun.

In the savanna, chimps often stop to look for predators before they walk across an open area.

In a rain forest, chimps spend a lot of their time in the leafy treetops.

Chimps are very strong. Some have the strength of several adult humans. They are also excellent climbers. To get somewhere quickly, they sometimes swing from branch to branch. However, chimps usually move around on the ground. They can walk upright, but they usually walk on all fours, using the knuckles of their hands and the soles of their feet.

Chimps' fingers and toes can curl firmly around trunks and branches. Their big toes are like our thumbs, and they help chimps grip things.

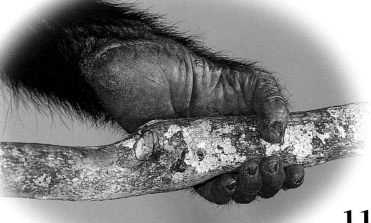

11

What is a troop's territory?

Each troop of chimps lives in an area that has the things they need. This area is called a **territory**. It is large enough to provide food and shelter for all the troop members. In **savanna habitats,** food plants can be far apart, so chimps have to move around to find food. Savanna territories can reach 77 square miles (200 square kilometers). That is equal to the area of about 37 football fields. Rain forest territories are just a tenth of this size, because food can be found more easily there.

Knowing Your Territory

Different troops of chimps often have territories next to each other. Sometimes they overlap slightly, but usually there is a chimp-free area between them. Territory edges are not always easy to spot, but chimps know where they are by remembering landmarks, such as a large rock, and by seeing or listening to the calls of chimps from other troops.

Where do chimps sleep?

Chimps do not always sleep in the same place. Instead, when they stop at the end of a busy day, they build new nests in nearby trees.

Each chimp makes its own nest at dusk. Mothers make one large enough for themselves and their young. Chimps make their nests high up in leafy trees where **predators**, such as leopards, cannot see them. Even if they are noticed, the chimps have a good chance of escaping. They can jump from tree to tree.

Chimps make nests by bending over large branches and then weaving smaller ones to make a flat basket. They put leafy branches inside to make a sort of mattress. After a good night's sleep, chimps abandon their nests and move off to find their first meal of the day.

Chimps practice nest making when they are young by watching and copying their mothers.

13

What Do Chimpanzees Eat?

All chimpanzees are **omnivores.** They eat mostly fruit, but they also eat the nuts, leaves, bark, and stems of hundreds of types of plants. They also eat meat from other animals they catch, including **insects.**

Chimps move around their **territories** alone or in small groups, looking for food. Sometimes they use special calls to invite other troop members to join them if they find a tree full of ripe fruit. If they find smaller amounts of food, they often keep it to themselves.

Chimps are so smart that they remember what time of year the fruit of different trees is ripe and ready to eat. They also remember where the different kinds of trees are. Then the chimps know when and where to go to get their favorite foods.

Chimps may eat for up to six hours each day. They get most of the water they need from the fruit they eat.

Hunters

Some groups of males hunt small mammals, such as antelope. These chimps **cooperate** by taking different jobs in the hunt. Some chase the **prey** through the forest, others block its escape. The **dominant** male catches and kills the **prey**, and the troop fights over the meat.

Using tools

Baby chimps learn how to get food by watching other chimps. Many chimps use tools to help them get food. Some pull leaves off twigs to make a stick. They poke the stick into **termite** or ant nests to reach the insects. Others use stones to crack hard nuts or chew a handful of leaves to make a "sponge" to soak up drinking water from hollow trees.

A chimp uses a stick to get termites out of their nest. The termites grab onto the stick and the chimp scrapes them off with his mouth. If he used his fingers, the termites would bite him.

15

How Do Chimps Care for Their Young?

Female chimpanzees are **pregnant** for eight months before they give birth. They normally have a single baby that weighs around 3.3 pounds (1.5 kilograms). As they grow up, young chimpanzees learn about life from their parents and from the other chimps around them. Just like human children, they are cared for over many years before they have to look after themselves.

Chimp Facts of Life

Chimps can **mate** at any time of year. Females usually start to have babies when they are about thirteen years old and may have a new baby every five years. Males are often fifteen years old before they are important enough in the troop for females to want to mate with them. Males usually show little interest in their young.

A mother carries her new baby for several days after it is born until it is strong enough to cling to her belly as she walks. When the baby gets a bit older, it will ride on her back.

Growing up in a troop

When a baby chimp is born, other chimps in the troop are interested in the new arrival. But the mother keeps them away from the baby for about six months. She does this to protect the baby, especially from **adolescent** males who might handle it roughly and hurt it.

Young chimps depend on their mother's milk for two years. They can also eat soft food, such as fruit, which she gives them during this time. Some young keep **suckling** even when they can find their own food.

After about six years, young chimps start to spend some time away from their mothers. They often form all male or all female gangs and wander around. Sometimes several days go by before they return to their mothers.

The friendships between young males in a troop become stronger as they work together, hunting for food and fighting nearby troops.

Do Chimps Talk to Each Other?

It is very important for chimpanzees to share information. This is known as **communication**. They need to let others know about food, danger, and how they feel, so their troop can stick together.

Chimps are very noisy animals that communicate using sound. They use up to 32 different calls. A loud "wraaaa" means a chimp has found something unusual or dangerous. A cough or squeak means it is nervous. A whimper means it is unhappy, and a "huh" sound means it is confused.

The pant-hoot

The **pant-hoot** is a call that all chimps make. Each chimp's pant-hoot is slightly different, so chimps can use it to identify other members of their troop. It tells other chimps where a certain chimp is, even if he or she cannot be seen.

Sometimes chimps drum against trees when they pant-hoot to make sure they can be heard a long way away.

Body language

A lot of chimp communication relies on body language. This is the way people and animals use their body to help them communicate, such as the look on their face, the way they are standing, or what they are doing with their hands. For example, for chimps, a wide, toothy grin is not a smile. This means it is nervous or afraid.

Talking to Humans?

Chimps cannot talk the way humans do. In zoos and wildlife parks, though, some chimps have learned to communicate with people. Some have learned the meanings of over 150 words in sign language. Others have learned how to tap messages onto special keyboards.

When greeting a **dominant** chimp, a less important chimp often grins, crouches, and holds a hand out. The dominant chimp may then welcome the other one by touching or kissing it on the face or by giving it a hug.

How Do Chimpanzees Relax?

Chimpanzees usually take a rest in the heat of the day. They often relax or snooze in day nests that they build on the ground or up in a tree. They make these day nests with less care than sleeping nests. But they still need to make the nests well enough to keep them dry in case of a heavy rain.

During rest times, chimps often **groom** each other, sometimes for several hours. Chimps like being groomed, so they do a favor for another chimp by grooming it. Apart from keeping clean, grooming is a way of becoming a better friend with another chimp or helping it to relax. It is also a friendly way of reminding everyone how important they are to the troop.

This chimp's strong toes grip onto a branch while it relaxes in a tree.

Playing around

When their mothers are busy grooming other chimps, young chimps like to play. Chimps seem to play just for the fun of it. Favorite group games are tag and king of the hill. If one chimp starts a game, others will soon join in. Playing is also an important way of practicing things the young chimps will need to do when they are older.

Chimps make a special face when they play. They show their lower teeth, and make a hoarse, panting sound like laughter.

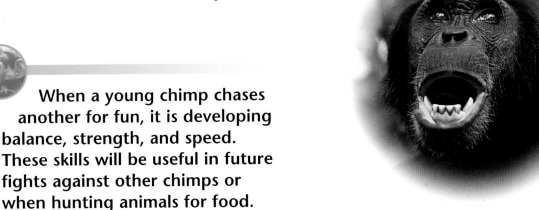

When a young chimp chases another for fun, it is developing balance, strength, and speed. These skills will be useful in future fights against other chimps or when hunting animals for food.

21

Do Chimps in a Troop Argue?

Chimps are a lot like people. They often have arguments about things such as food, friends, and who is best at something. Many arguments in a troop are very short and, after a bit of screaming, everyone calms down. Some arguments, though, can quickly turn into fights, particularly between adult males. Male chimps are strong and have sharp teeth, so chimps can get badly hurt in a fight. To avoid this, chimps have ways of preventing too many fights in a troop.

A **dominant** male chimp often shows how important he is by using special behavior called **displays.** He makes lots of noise by screaming, slapping his hands, and stamping his feet. He shows how strong he is by charging around, dragging branches as he runs, or throwing heavy rocks. He shows how big he is by standing up on two legs, waving his arms, and making his hair stand up.

This male chimp is displaying by tearing up and shaking plants.

Fighting

By displaying, the dominant male reminds other chimps how well he could fight if he wanted to. This stops many males from trying to replace him as the dominant chimp. If other males still want to fight him, they display in the same way. Displaying can quickly turn into a fight. The males charge one another, then slap and bite each other as hard as they can. Females pick up their young to get them out of the way.

Fights are often short. The losing chimp runs or creeps away, often screaming, and hides until things calm down. Then he returns to the troop, crouching and panting. To show that he accepts that he has lost, he grooms others in the troop—especially the male who won the fight.

Male chimps have long teeth that can badly hurt other chimps. Often, they can avoid fights just by showing their teeth.

23

Does a Troop Ever Change?

The importance of chimps in a troop changes as time passes. Younger males grow bigger and stronger. The **dominant** male gets older and weaker. Eventually, he becomes too weak to **display** or fight well. He may even get hurt in fighting or die as a result of wounds. Then the troop needs a new leader. The strongest of the younger males fight. The one who wins becomes the new dominant male.

Getting older

Most dominant males are between 20 and 30 years old. This is the time in their lives when most chimps are at their strongest. When a male is too old and weak to be the dominant chimp, he begins to spend a lot of his time alone. He is still part of the troop, but he is no longer the center of things.

Moving on

Male chimps remain in the same troop as their mother for their whole lives, but females do not. When they are between eight to ten years old, young females leave to join other troops. At first, a female chimp spends more and more time with groups of young males from her own troop. Later, she meets males from a different troop and leaves for good.

A troop takes some time to get used to the new arrival. Members of the troop sometimes will not share food with her. There may even be fighting over where in her new troop's **territory** the female can get food. Eventually, most new females are accepted and can **mate** with males in the troop.

Most female chimps do not stay in the troop into which they were born. So, the adult females in a troop are usually not related.

What Dangers Does a Troop Face?

One of the worst dangers a troop faces is an attack by male chimps from another troop. Males sometimes attack to take over more **territory** and the food it contains. A single male may attack a troop to try to become its new leader. This is why chimps treat any males from other troops as dangerous enemies.

Sometimes groups of males from one troop sit quietly on the edge of their territory, listening and looking into the neighboring territory. When they see a large group of enemy chimps, they **pant-hoot** and **display.** If they spot an enemy male on his own, the group will chase him. If they capture the male, they usually hurt him so badly that he dies. In some troops of chimps there are far fewer males than females because of fighting like this.

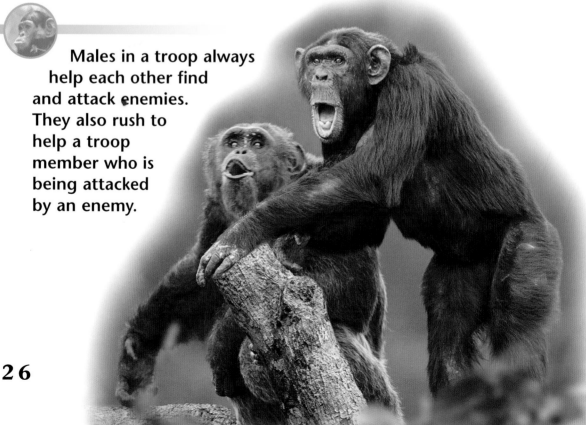

Males in a troop always help each other find and attack enemies. They also rush to help a troop member who is being attacked by an enemy.

Not Enough Food

Since a lot of the food chimps eat grows wild, how much there is changes from year to year. The amount depends on the weather and how many animals are eating the food. When there is not much food, chimps need to travel farther to find it. This often causes fights over territory.

Dangers from other animals

Chimpanzees do not have many natural **predators**. However, leopards and lions sometimes catch, kill, and eat chimps, especially young, old, or weak ones. The most dangerous animals for chimps are people. Some people hunt chimps and sell them as food. People sometimes kill mother chimps to take their babies, which they sell or keep as pets.

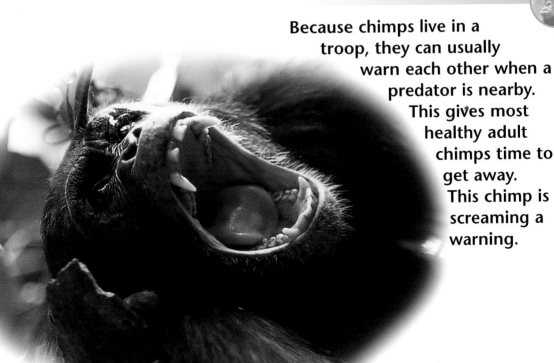

Because chimps live in a troop, they can usually warn each other when a predator is nearby. This gives most healthy adult chimps time to get away. This chimp is screaming a warning.

27

Nowhere to live

The biggest danger to chimp troops is the loss of the **habitats** in which they live. There are more and more people living in Africa today. To make space for their roads, farms, and buildings, people are cutting down lots of trees. This means that some of the areas of **rain forest** and **savanna** where chimps live are now only large enough for small troops of chimps.

A happy ending?

Conservation and research groups are working hard to protect chimps. They create protected areas of land where chimps are safe and no one is allowed to cut down trees. These groups are also trying to ban the hunting of chimps. Hopefully, chimp troops will soon be left alone to live safe, healthy lives.

These workers at a research center give chimps extra food because they cannot find enough food in their **territory**.

Chimpanzee Facts

Where do chimps live?

This map shows where most of the chimpanzees in the world live today. Chimps live in the area colored green on this map.

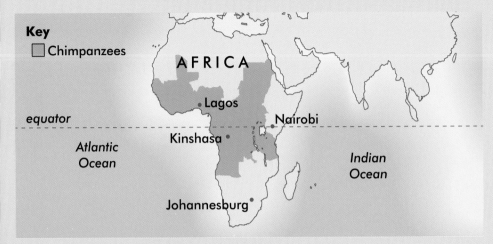

Key
☐ Chimpanzees

AFRICA

• Lagos

equator

Nairobi

Kinshasa •

Atlantic
Ocean

Indian
Ocean

Johannesburg •

Are chimps disappearing?

About 50 years ago there were several million chimps in Africa. Now there are only about 200,000.

What tools do chimps use?

Chimps use about 26 different tools for finding and eating food. The only animals to use more tools are humans. Chimps also use stones and sticks as weapons to throw at baboons to chase them away from their food. Some chimps use leaves like napkins or tissues to wipe their sticky lips and hands after eating.

What do chimps eat?

A large, male chimp can eat 50 bananas in one sitting. Some males eat up to 55 pounds (25 kilograms) of meat each day. Favorite chimp foods are grapes, figs, and the nuts of palm trees. They also love to eat honey made by wild bees. Chimps travel up to 7 miles (11 kilometers) every day looking for food.

Glossary

adaptation   special feature that allows living things to survive in their particular habitat

adolescent   describes the time when an animal is nearly an adult

communicate   pass on information to another

conservation   taking action to protect living things and their habitat

cooperate   help each other

display   put on a show of actions that sends a message to another animal

dominant   refers to the leader or the most important member of a group

equator   imaginary line around the middle of Earth

grooming   when one animal cleans bits of dirt, dead skin, or insects from the hair of another animal

habitat   place where an animal or plant lives in the wild

insect   small, six-legged animal with a body divided into three sections: the head, thorax, and abdomen

jaw   moving part of the skull that opens and closes the mouth

mammal   warm-blooded, hairy animal. Mammal babies grow inside the mother. The mother cares for the babies after they are born and they drink her milk.

mate   joining of a male and female of the same species to create young

omnivore   animal that eats both animals and plants

pant-hoot   special loud call that all chimps make

pecking order   order of importance of animals in a group. The highest member in the pecking order is the leader.

predator   animal that hunts other animals for food

pregnant   when a mother has a baby growing inside her, before it is born

prey   animal that is hunted and eaten by another animal

rain forest   thick forest of tall trees that grows in hot, sunny places where it rains almost every day

savanna   large, open area of land mostly covered with grasses but with patches of woodland

social   living in well-organized groups of animals that work together

species   group of living things that are alike in many ways and can mate to produce young

suckling   when a baby animal is drinking milk from its mother

termites   insects, similar to ants, that eat wood and sometimes live in tall mud nests

territory   particular area that an animal or group of animals claims as its own

More Books to Read

Banks, Martin. *Chimpanzee: Habitats, Life Cycles, Food Chains, Threats*. Austin, Tex.: Raintree, 2000.

Farbman, Melinda and Frye Gaillard. *Spacechimp: NASA's Ape in Space*. Berkeley Heights, N.J.: Enslow Publishers, 2000.

Goodall, Jane. *The Chimpanzee Family Book*. New York: North South Books, 1997.

Kratt, Chris and Martin Kratt. *Kratts' Creatures: To Be a Chimpanzee*. New York: Scholastic Trade, 1997.

Nagda, Anne Whitehead and Cindy Bickel. *Chimp Math*. New York: Henry Holt, 2002.

Index